The author, Nadjmat Abdoulhakime, studied accounting and finance and has 18 years of work experience. Her current position, at the time of this book being published, is the Commercial Consul of Comoros Islands in the United Arab Emirates.

Her personal and professional experiences living in different countries played a major role in influencing her mindset and lifestyle. She was born in Comoros, then moved to Paris where she grew up, and had the opportunity to move to Dubai soon after starting her career to work for an American corporation. She then moved to the US and subsequently spent a year of volunteering in Indonesia where she helped create her first financial literacy book.

Her first company was a coffee restaurant. She started at a very young age with some of her cousins. Her childhood environment shaped her perspective of money, entrepreneurship, and embracing new challenges. She recognizes that financial literacy is a subject that is often never taught neither at school nor at home. Most education curriculums do not cover this topic while being a crucial aspect of our lives. Money and relationships to money is key to one's independence and freedom. Learning about money will always be beneficial and contribute to a healthier financial lifestyle.

NADJMAT ABDOULHAKIME

# MY FIRST BANK ACCOUNT

## Austin Macauley Publishers™
LONDON • CAMBRIDGE • NEW YORK • SHARJAH

Copyright © Nadjmat Abdoulhakime 2024

The right of **Nadjmat Abdoulhakime** to be identified as author of this work has been asserted by the author in accordance with Federal Law No. (7) of UAE, Year 2002, Concerning Copyrights and Neighboring Rights.

All rights reserved. No part of this publication may be reproduced, stored in a retrieval system, or transmitted in any form or by any means, electronic, mechanical, photocopying, recording, or otherwise, without the prior permission of the publishers.

Any person who commits any unauthorized act in relation to this publication may be liable to legal prosecution and civil claims for damages.

ISBN – 9789948752875 – (Paperback)
ISBN – 9789948752882 – (E-Book)

Application Number: MC-10-01-5907275
Age Classification: E

The age group that matches the content of the books has been classified according to the age classification system issued by the UAE Media Council.

Printer Name: iPrint Global Ltd
Printer Address: Witchford, England

First Published 2024
AUSTIN MACAULEY PUBLISHERS FZE
Sharjah Publishing City
P.O. Box [519201]
Sharjah, UAE
www.austinmacauley.ae
+971 655 95 202

This book is dedicated to my beloved parents, Abdoulhakime Allaoui and Soiffat Bourhane, for their endless love, support, and encouragement. I owe my parents everything! And also, to my beloved brothers, Nahyane and Hirmane, and their families for their generous love and support that they have provided me throughout my entire life.

First and foremost, I must acknowledge my limitless thanks to Allah, the Ever-Magnificent, the Ever-Thankful, for His help and giving me the opportunity, courage, and enough energy to carry out and complete this book, *My First Bank Account*, part of a series of 4 books on Financial Literacy.

The Gardeners, Adam, Chloe and their four kids, live in a nice neighborhood. Adam and Chloe have been married for 15 years. Their oldest son, Dan, is 14. Their twins, Leah and Joel, are 12, and their youngest daughter, Hope, is 10.

Adam is an entrepreneur and has always been a business owner. He grew up in a family where working was essential. Adam is a home renovator, an architect, and a designer. He works with multiple people and has built his reputation on several successful projects he achieved during the five years of running his business. His dad inspired him to grow his career in home renovation and he loves it!

Chloe is also an entrepreneur. She is a stay-at-home mom who homeschools her kids and, at the same time, runs her tea company. She has her own YouTube channel and has been selling tea for two years. She loves herbs and has found a way to grow them and create her own combinations. Her company has a lot of success in her community, and in local shops that love her beautiful designs and her homemade concoctions.

On Mondays, the Gardeners usually focus on their administrative tasks. Chloe has always had a good routine with her kids. She combines homeschooling with external activities daily. She makes sure she teaches them theoretical subjects and gives them time to practice life with the community and participate in the house.

Adam usually goes to the bank on Monday mornings for cash and cheque deposits. He often goes on his own but sometimes asks Dan to accompany him. Dan happens to be free and goes with his dad to the bank on that day.

Adam is pleased to be bonding more with his son. Adam and Chloe want their kids to focus on knowing more about business and money.

They have always been open in talking about work and now was the time for them to involve the kids in the practical way of making and managing money.

Adam: Dan, I want to leave in 15 minutes. Is that okay with you?

Dan: Yes, Dad. I'm ready.

Adam and Dan get ready, put their shoes on and get into the car.

The bank is downtown, which is 15 minutes away from their house

Adam and Dan arrive at the bank. They approach the bank teller and greet her.

Bank teller: Good morning, Mr. Gardener. How are you today?

Adam: Good morning, madam, I am doing very well. How about you?

Bank teller: I am doing fantastic. How can I help you today?

Adam: I would like to deposit $5000 into my company bank account, please.

Bank teller: Of course, please fill out this deposit slip.

Adam: Here you are. I have filled out the slip and signed it.

Bank teller: Great. Here is a receipt for your deposit.

Adam: Thank you! Could I also get my bank balance printed as of today?

Bank teller: Absolutely! Here is your bank balance, Mr. Gardner.

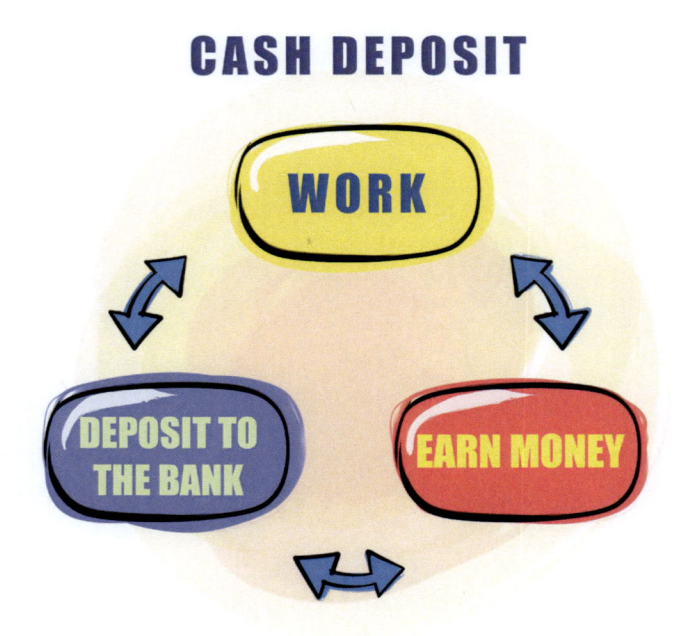

**CASH DEPOSIT**

WORK

DEPOSIT TO THE BANK

EARN MONEY

Adam completes the transaction and turns to Dan to leave when Dan interrupts him.

Dan: Dad, I would like to have my own bank account. I know you and Mom give us cash as pocket money, but I would love to have a bank account to deposit the money I have.

Adam: You are right. That is a great suggestion. A bank account is a safe place to keep your money.

Dan: I have money at home but if I open the bank account today, maybe next Monday, I can come back with you and deposit my money.

Adam: That is a great idea, Dan. Let us ask the bank teller what we need to open your own bank account and if you have all you need, we can do it now.

Adam turns to the bank teller.

Adam: Madam, I would like to know what documents are required to open a bank account for my son who's 14?

Bank teller: Sure thing. That's a great idea! The bank requires, your approval or your spouse's approval given your son's age, and his Social Security number along with a proper form of I.D.

**Document needed to open a bank account as a teenager.**

Adam turns to his son.

Adam: Do you have these documents with you?

Dan: Yes. Here they are.

Adam: Fantastic. Why don't you do the process with the bank teller? I will step out and let you continue. If you need me, I am here to sign any form required.

Dan approaches the bank teller and continues the process with her.

Bank teller: Hello, young man, how are you? How can I help you today?

Dan: Hello, madam, I think you just talked to my dad, and I would like to open a bank account, please.

Bank teller: Absolutely. We will need your parents' permission, so your dad will need to sign a consent form. Then, we will be ready to proceed.
Dan turns to his dad.

Dan: Dad, can you please sign this form for me?

Adam signs the form and hands it to Dan.

Dan: Here it is, madam. Here is my SSN and ID, too.

A few minutes later, the bank teller turns to Dan.

Bank teller: Congratulations, Mr. Gardener. You have now opened your bank account. We are very happy to have you as a new customer. Your checking account will help you learn how to check your balance, set up direct deposits, use ATMs, use a debit card, budget, and transfer money. The card will be sent to your parents' home address in the next few days.

Dan: Thank you so much. That's fantastic news.

Dan turns to his dad very excited and proud.

Dan: It is done, Dad.

Adam: Congratulations, son. I am very proud of you. You are the best.

On their way home, Dan asks his dad more details about the bank account and the information the bank teller told him.

**Purpose of a bank/checking account**

Dan: Thank you, Dad, for helping me opening my bank account and supporting my suggestion. I'm so happy to have a bank account now.

Adam: My pleasure, son! I'm proud of you for asking. Your mom and I have talked about getting you kids more involved in understanding money, and I believe that this is an amazing way to start.

Dan: I see many banks around. How long have you been with this bank, and why did you choose this one?

Adam: Excellent questions, son. Grandpa has been with this bank for a long time and has built a great relationship with them. Same as you, he opened my bank account with them when I was a teenager. I believe I was around 17. I like it because of the great relationship we have that took years to build.

Dan: That's amazing, Dad! What do you like the most about it?

Adam: I like the fact that it is a mutual bank. The customer service is excellent. They always make me feel like my success is the bank's success. Employees do their best to ensure that I am well served and informed. The other thing I love is that profits are reinvested in the community. The bank donates to local schools, cultural places, and community events a lot.

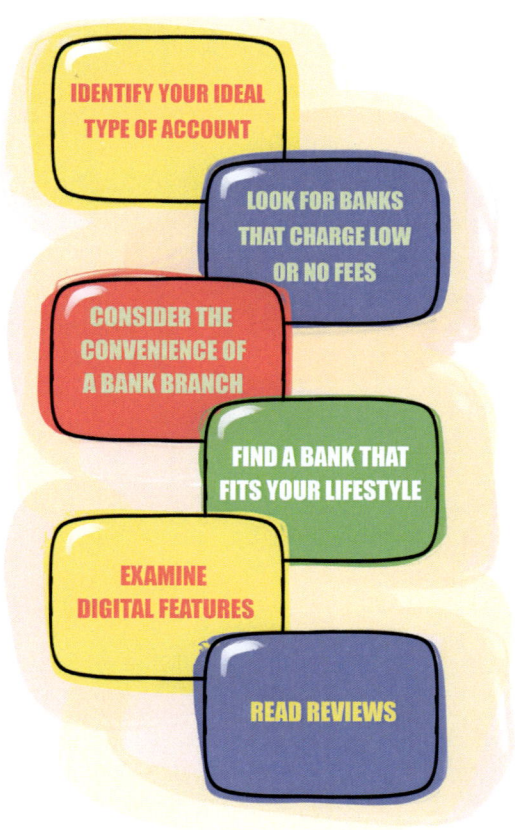

**How to choose a bank**

Dan: Oh wow, Dad! I did not know that. That is indeed amazing.

Adam: Absolutely. Money happens when you focus on people.

Dan: The teller said that I will get my debit card in a few days. What is the difference between a debit card and a credit card? I've heard you talk about a credit card before.

Adam: Excellent question, son. A debit card is a card used as a payment method to cash when buying things. You can only use a debit card when you have money in your bank account as opposed to a credit card, which is used to borrow money. It is a card with which a person can buy things and pay for them later. So, most people, who use a credit card, very often, do not have the cash to pay for what they are buying at the time of the purchase.

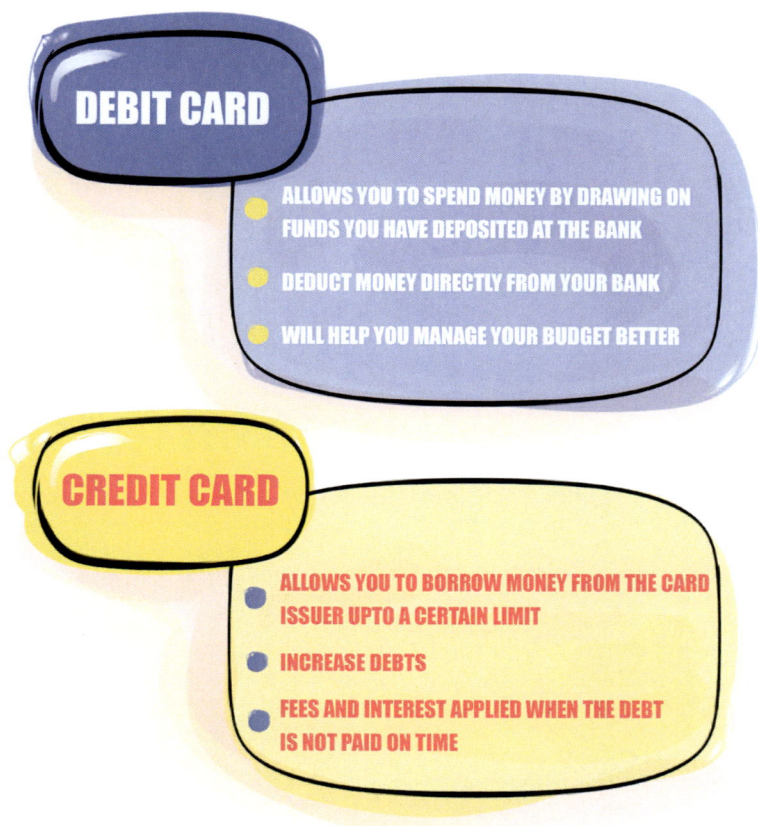

**Debit Card vs. Credit Card**

Dan: Which card is better? Which one do you use the most?

Adam: My rule is: if I cannot pay cash, then I cannot afford it. So, my favorite is always the debit card. But a credit card and borrowing money, done wisely, is also a good option to have and consider sometimes. But always remember to think of what you can afford and then pay for it.

## Vocabulary and definition:

* **Bank:** A place to keep everyone's money safe.
* **Bank account:** A place to keep your money safe.
* **Bank Teller:** An employee of a bank that hands customer's cash and money transactions.
* **Business:** A place to sell goods or services.

* **Cash:** Cash is the physical form of money.
* **Community:** A place near where you live and where people know each other.
* **Credit card:** Card that is used to borrow money when buying things. A card with which a person can buy things and pay for them later.

* **Deposit:** Put something into a place.
* **Debit card:** Card that is used as a payment method to cash when buying things.
* **Donation:** Something given to help those in need a donation to charity.

* **Document:** A piece of written, printed, or electronic matter that provides information or evidence or that serves as an official record.

* **Identity (I.D):** A document used to verify a person's identity.
* **Investment:** The act of putting out money in order to gain a profit.

* **Money:** An item to buy things.
* **Mutual Bank:** A state-chartered savings bank owned by its depositors and managed by a board of trustees.

* **Profit:** To get some good out of something, gain something.

* **Relationships:** The state of being related or connected.

* **Service:** An act of helpful activity.
* **Social Security Number (SSN):** It is a number issued to person citizens of that country.
* **Success:** To have a good or favorable result, do well.

"Praised be Allah, Who, whenever He is thanked for one of His blessings, provides another blessing which in turn obliges one to thank Him again!"

# THE END